TWO JOURNALS

JAMES
SCHUYLER

DARRAGH
PARK

Introduction by Douglas Crase

Tibor de Nagy Editions   New York   1995

First edition published in 1995 by

Tibor de Nagy Editions
41 West 57th Street
New York, NY 10019

The complete journals of James Schuyler are being
edited by Nathan Kernan for future publication.

Library of Congress Catalog Card Number: 95-061538
ISBN 0-9639033-4-9

All drawings are graphite on Arches text laid paper, 11 ¾ x 8 ¼ in.

FIRST EDITION

PREFACE

In 1985 James Schuyler and I decided to keep accompanying journals which would not, however, be mutually descriptive.

The resulting entries - written and drawn, and presented here in chronological order - dealt with subjects we discussed during our Sunday telephone calls, dinners and visits: the view from the Hotel Chelsea, the fate of the Mets, painting in Ocean City, Md. and Miami, doctor appointments, motorcycle travel, dog news, cat news, the summer landscape, television viewing, reminiscences, work progress, records played, a concert attended, the bathroom sink.

Much of this constituted raw material for the work of us both, often finding expression later in poems and paintings. These journals are thus not only in some way an account of our relationship but also evidence of some of the things which nourished our creative lives.

— D.P.

INTRODUCTION

When James Schuyler presented in a poem his now famous instructions for teaching people to write poetry, he did not exactly come clean. "Oh forget it," he wrote. "Reading / writing, knowing other poets/ will do it, if there is/ anything doing." To be true to his own example he should have added that knowing painters is also a good idea. His writing life was rich in poet-painter friendships, and pre-eminent among them in the fifteen years before he died in 1991 was his friendship with Darragh Park.

It was a lucky match. Schuyler is routinely identified as a poet of the New York School, that creative misnomer bestowed through the Tibor de Nagy Gallery on poets known in the 1950's not for a common style, but for their ties to the then emerging world of New York painters. In that world, Schuyler's loyalties had been to the painterly realists. Park's artistic lineage runs through those same painters; but Park, a generation younger, could approach their successes as achieved tradition, something to assimilate and transume. Inevitably, the poet was to observe this younger painter test the very tradition in which the poet's own art had origins. The lesson must have been difficult to avoid.

Park reached for the premonitory edges that painterly realism sometimes had left aside. Schuyler stretched his lines to accommodate, barely, the racing perceptions of event-troped poems. The poet admitted "eye gunk" to the lyric vocabulary; the painter welcomed the unembarassed physics of ballparks and beachfront real estate. Their twofold *Two Journals* became at the same time a work of art and a witness of reciprocal encouragement, occasion alone to reinaugurate the legendary Tibor de Nagy Editions that from 1951 to 1970 helped define what is liveliest in the exchange between painting and poetry. One measure indeed of its charm, and artistry, is how *Two Journals* manages to imply that artistic courage is something we all might enjoy as human property, though

9

unavailable until the friendship comes along in which we can pass it back and forth, and keep it, so to speak, in play.

Poets and painters have been excessively praised, then criticized, for studying daily life, as if thus they were proved perceptually servile to weather, the *Times*, and the status quo. The praise and criticism alike assume that there really is a daily life, and that anyone actually lives it in a world now multiply redefined and daily on the move. For those who are not so sure, there is a certain satisfaction in discovering that Park, a motorcyclist, kept Schuyler apprised throughout their collaboration of his reorienting experiences on the road. Park once remarked on the importance of focusing well ahead of his speed in order not to get killed, and added drily: "The rest of my vision had to and did take in everything." That deadpan addendum could be the credo for Schuyler's later poems and Park's own recent oils and watercolors. It describes a standard that gives *Two Journals,* too, its tugging appeal. These day-to-day sketches and diaries are the first forward attention to perceptions so unstable, so rapidly passing on all sides, that only the artist's focus has popped them out of probability and into view. Each focus has the pulse of rescue. Each stirs a wake of desire as wide as the rest of vision that, meanwhile, took in everything. The *everything* is what these artists have begun to restore, in work that will detain us widely enough to reveal how daily life is the most metaphysical thing we do.

— Douglas Crase

11

TWO JOURNALS

Winter seems to go on and on—and here it is, only a little more than three weeks into it! And I used to love cold and snow so much. Perhaps everything seems better in the country.

Tom is coming over this afternoon (perhaps) —what with the play he's in and his working, I see him hardly at all. If he's ever in a Broadway hit, as he no doubt will be one day, I'll go bananas. But if he's in a hit, I suppose he wouldn't have to go on working at Joe Allen's. That might be a gain?

Now to get ready for Hy Weitzen—shave, shower, wash my hair. Surprise, I already have! So I can spend a couple of hours with the depressing last volume of Virginia's diary. Such a waste! Poor lovely lady.

More snow, small flakes, falling criss-cross on themselves. And tonight it's supposed to hit zero! "Supposed" means that was the prediction on the 11 o'clock news last night by Channel 4's Al Roker.

A Clint Eastwood Americana type comedy (I guess) about boxing and the mob. Let's face it: the great Clint is no comic genius, and why at his age do they keep featuring him with his shirt off? On the other hand, an actor named William Smith (I think) is quite a hunk: a delectable hunk.

But I meant to say in my weather report, the east French window is up to its usual winter tricks. At the coldest part of a really cold night, something freezes and contracts, and the window pops open. One night this week the temperature hit 14, and when I woke up, about 7:30, it was 14 indoors as well as out! Last year I remember propping a chair against it. Time to start that anew, I guess. Mostly, this place is heavily over heated indeed, and I have to open the window.

John Ashbery got the Bollingen prize. I've never begrudged John one jot (or tittle) of his success and honors: he deserves them all and I applaud. But once, just once, I'd like to get one of these prizes first—then I'd like it to be instantly given to John. But I don't think there are any left, except the Nobel, and who's worrying about that? Still, the Nobel is a nice hunk of cash.

The pink and white tyranny of a sunny, well-snowed upon February morning. At least we don't hear the dreaded words, "sleet, changing to freezing rain." Just pink sunlight, blue sky, whitest of white snow.

Back, three days ago, from another week at Beekman hospital. Pneumonia this time: "If anybody asks you," Daniel Newman said, "you just had plain pneumonia, not any other kind." I didn't get it at first, but somebody down there is always trying to foist an AIDS diagnosis on me: at least two guys put in my chart that I had the very much wrong kind of pneumonia: the kind that lately killed America's leading female impersonator, "Mr. Lynn Carter."

But that hospital: I don't even want to hear its name, much less go near it!

Helena had had the flu all week, so Bill de Noyelles had been working for me. What a find that boy is! He's so prompt and capable, and a pleasure to have around.

His birthday, and the day after Wystan Auden's. It was always nice that there was a holiday. The day after Wystan's annual birthday: a clear space in which to nurse one's hangover! The great no drinking bonus: no more hangovers. How they used to wreck my life.

At Six AM the heavy gray burns a heavier blue. Rain, water drops clinging to the balcony.

Back yesterday from a week at Beekman Downtown hospital. This time, aspirin poisoning — I overdosed. So now I'm cut to one tablet a day, forever and ever.

Tom came to see me in the hospital last Monday, and again yesterday morning. What a good boy! I do love him.

And that nice Jimmy McCourt has put me into *Kaye Wayfering in Avenged*; well not me, quotes from "Hymn to Life." Just where I'd like it to be. Such a talented lad.

And I feel good.

I dreamed I was trying to reassure John A. about the danger of riding the subway. His main concern was about lead-based paint flaking off and getting into his food. I told him I understood the subway had been freshly painted, but he wasn't buying that. Then I said I didn't think they used lead-based paint anymore: but he wasn't buying that either. All in all, I didn't do too well.

And now I'm having dinner with John tomorrow night—for the first time in how long?

And now off to see Hy Weitzen and try to make sense of my aspirin OD.

"A Cold Spring" is what we're having: we're honoring Elizabeth Bishop's memory.

A very pleasant get together with John A., Darragh and Joe Brainard on Wednesday night. John's gorgeous new apartment is only $675 a month! Views to Jersey. We ate at a tiny restaurant around the corner at 21st and 8th Avenue called (I think), Onini's. Good, though not so good as Lombardi's: but a hell of a lot handier than Spring and Mulberry. Of the foursome I, though the oldest, was the least grey: I like that: a year ago I expected to be snow white by now. And what did the assembled beauty queens talk about? AIDS, of course.

The other night, consumed with ennui, for the first time in my life I watched a baseball game from start to finish: the All-Stars game from Minneapolis. I like the way the players are always groping themselves (do they all have jock itch?) and slapping each other on the butt. But my *pash*, Gary Carter, the catcher for the Mets, had an inflamed knee and couldn't play. But there were plenty of other hunks, although Goose Gossage, I'm afraid, "is not fair to outward view."

Oh. There is a famous Florentine portrait of a man with a diseased nose — swollen and pitted —with his little son or grandson. On the train coming back last night for the first time I saw a man who suffered from that condition, so much so that it was painful to look at him. Deformity doesn't usually bother me, but this, I'm sorry to say, really got to me. One would imagine plastic surgery could do something about it. But how would I know? I pitied him.

Tuesday, bloody Tuesday. Now why do I say that? And what business of yours is it how I feel about Tuesday? Hmmmm?

It's getting light out, grey-blue-grey. And the parlor linden Darragh gave me now o'er tops the French windows. It has an alarming amount of leaf drop; but Darragh assures me that's the nature of the beast.

I know why it's bloody Tuesday: no giant lime tree, no butter nut tree, no pond, no Tom, no Darragh...

I don't understand the motions of the sun: I thought it never shone into north-facing rooms, but every morning, soon after rising, it illuminates the recesses of my two French windows. But mostly I live, as I read in Diego Giacometti's obituary, "in a town into which the sun did not shine three months of the year."

How often I wake up feeling that I'd like to write a poem, but no words come of my own into my mind: those that do are Vaughn's:

> They are all gone into the world of light
>
> And I alone sit lingering here
>
> Their very memory is clear and bright
>
> And my sad thought doth clear

And I wonder how accurate that is? Me memory for poetry is zilch.

Yesterday is a day I'm not going to think about, much less discuss. Enough to say, I was as cross as two sticks.

Is it possible my favorite poem is Coleridge's "Frost at Midnight?" It may be true, and if it isn't, so what?

Yesterday I said I wanted to write a poem but couldn't. Later I took a nap (that great institution), woke up and wrote one, lay down to read and got up another. I suspect both of being stinkers and have no inclination to look at them right now. And yet, there are those pleasant, if rare, occasions when what had seemed designed by a Higher Power for the ash can turns out not to be not so far below the norm as all that. It never hurts to keep one's hand in, and there have to be rifts before you start loading them with gold. Or is the word ore?

I'm still pissed off, but for different reasons - or for the old reasons plus new ones. Forget it. I wish I could.

I wish I had one hundred brand new books to read.

Sweet Catullus' *all but island, olive silvery Sirmio....*

When he felt like it, Wystan could set the cat among the pigeons: I remember a review in which Desmond McCarthy foamed, because W. had said — in print — that Tennyson was the most musical of English poets, and the stupidest.

I love Tennyson, and he is indeed most marvelously musical, but sometimes it seems a little Cecile Chaminade. Surely W. would not have stooped to guff about "the murmuring of immemorial elms"— or however it goes — elms which turned out not to be so immemorial after all.

For music, I prefer the vintage Keats bottled: "Season of mists and mellow fruitfulness..." Bright star! Indeed.

I was filled with delight last night —how disgusting, a rhyme—when I realized that anyone whoever wants to write my biography will have his/her work cut out for her/him, since virtually no documentation or juvenilia exist. There is The Birth Certificate, The First Grade Report Card (F in all subjects: I was a late bloomer), The Passport: and? No diplomas, no degrees, maybe some post cards and a letter or two...then I had three stories published in *Accent* along with Frank's "Three Penny Opera," the poem behind my poem, "Salute" (it's the matter of where the line turns), met John Ashbery, Jane Freilicher, Fairfield Porter, Edwin Denby, Rudy Burckhardt (through his sister, Helen), and other geniuses and the rest is history....

There is a hilarious piece in this week's *New Yorker* called "Yo, Poe." It concerns Sylvester Stallone's wish to play the *real* Poe who was *not* a kinky alcoholic —but the big stuff was Whitney Balliett's (*why* can't I spell that name?) piece on Peggy Lee, who is in town, around the corner, singing tonight, and I won't be there: you better believe I'm pissed off. But I am going to own and play her latest LP very, very soon. Goody. *The Sorcerer's Helper* begins to pall.

Virgil T. to Sauguet, issuing from a NY jazz club: *"Elle n'est-pas artiste,"* in definitive tones. They had been listening to Lady Day.

Edwin Denby told me that.

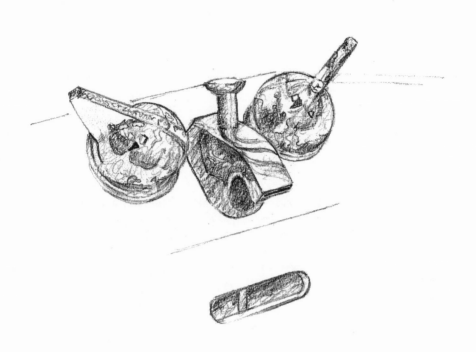

Brook Benton's "Do Your Own Thing" is just the music I want right now, and the three Teddy Wilson discs with Mildred Bailey (who once spoke to me at Cafe Society Uptown: "Take it easy Sonny," she said as I stumbled slightly on the stair [the can was upstairs] and swept down in a brown evening suit studded with brass nail beads and sang "Oh Mama Won't You Scrap Your Fat," and the boys stood up and joined her: it was a lovely lively number and then things got a lot better— nor will my day be ruined when Bill brings the latest Peggy Lee. Goody).

I watch *The Fabulous Dorsey Brothers* only because they were playing themselves: imagine my surprise when the words "with Helen O'Connell, Ziggy Elman, Bunny Berrigan, and other wizards: and Art Tatum." Art Tatum! It was true the plot of the movie is about how to prevent the audience from hearing any music: mostly it succeeded: then poster: "Art Tatum": eventually, Art Tatum, and was it beautiful: then authentic musicians stood and jammed. It was worth it.

Titles:

Pious Ejaculations

Inscrutable Wisdom Stone

The Master of the Controlled Accident

and others

While I was visiting my home-away-from-home for a brief stay —what Tom calls, "it's a retreat but it's not a religious retreat," only mine was and so was his so what's he talking about?—the parlor linden accomplished its appointed task: behind its spurious complaint of leaf-drop lay the disclosure of what Williams called "the alphabet of the trees" which now fills without hiding my west French window. A piece of wildness to live with: from what improbable jungle?

At the hour when sunlight steals in and coats the recessed paneling with glow, its leaves are transpicuous: big, light green, its branches rising from the base in an expanding errancy. Beyond and through: the urban clarity of rusticated stone and six-light windows, the Victorian fancy of chrysanthemums crudely reduced to iron: the balustrade of 'My' balcony.

Yestereve the sunset shone briefly— a long while it seemed — causing an effect in loft-style stately building across the way: a glow that reminded me of what happens in Venice when buckets of rain, including hail, fall upon Istrian stone: an inner pinkness that goes on and on and on until....

The Mystery plant (gift of George Schneeman in entertaining Schneeman flower pot) is doing nicely as is the sprig of ivy. The nearly dead from neglect and non-watering ("I have watered the plants": like hell you did) parlor linden that Darragh grew from a cutting is recovering nicely. It shed so many leaves that its skeleton shows plainly and attractively—"the alphabet of the trees." It stands on one of the speakers and needs turning. Why not now? Yes, now, while Ida Cox is singing: "Don't let your whiskey drive away your only friend."

Yesterday all hell broke loose. Forget it. Helena came back from Maine, air sick from a bumpy ride. She told me many Maine-Burckhardt stories. She was taken to see Edwin's grave in the woods where his ashes lie: an unmarked stone of no great size. Period. That elegance, that genius, that strange lover: and, aged eighty —why spell it out? He wrote his own epitaph when he looked at a photograph of the beautiful and great Nijinsky standing, one arm encircling his head, eyes closed: to Edwin it was,

"Mysterious as breathing in sleep..."

Dear heart, rest well.

A sunny day and Peggy Lee is singing and I wonder how dramatic today will be and quite possibly no drama at all. Not great sleep but some, always better than none.

Finances bug me: need clock from around corner ($15.00), need glasses with new frames ($45.00) anticipate Monday and Tuesday, cabs to Hy Weitzen and Dr. Newman (more or less $20) I suppose I can always give up food and live on air like an orchid. Oh. Well.

I like my new style poems very much , uncertain success of this morning's effort, a salute to Brook Benton. But I usually felt like that right after giving birth...

And very early in the night of the day it is: a phone call quite a while after I took my not all that effectual sleeping pill woke me up, but good. I didn't want the phone call, I made an arrangement I also particularly didn't want to make. Perhaps I do not confront life with the manliness, the virility I like to think I do: nowadays, at any rate.

One thing is clear: I confront the fact of my own inevitable death with indifference. Either what I believe is true -- the whole New Testament, and I have only read that in parts, particularly the gospel according to St.John -- but that doesn't matter. How much I have learned from knowing the prayers of the rosary, more or less memorizing the text of the Requiem, so beautiful, and right now I cannot remember the name of the great Italian poet who probably wrote it: attending mass with a missal and most of all going one morning with Anne to Our Lady of Poland. Such simplicity moves me more deeply than I can or need say. God bless you, Anne Elizabeth Channing Porter for all you have done for every one you love and for so many perhaps strangers!

To say that I am distressed by the death of that excellent actor, Rock Hudson! Dying prematurely of that horrendous ailment, AIDS, and with dignity and surrounded by his staff, his immediate family they were. I heard it on Live at Five on Channel 4, the whole hideous "and direct from in front of Rock Hudson's home in..." "Get that camera out of here you son of a bitch! What kind of people are you?" Not human, that's for sure. So I turned it off (enough is as good as a feast) and went by myself. Unconsoled? When so fine a man dies the question of personal consolation does not arise.

Now I like to think of him staying in his friend Elizabeth Taylor's apartment when he was last here in New York. I like to remember him in *Lili* with Julie Andrews, running around in a non-seduction scene in long undershorts, vintage World War I. And yet, what is there about comedies grounded in hideous wars that sometimes turns me off?

Now I must (or must not) address myself to the problem that Random House is no way about to reissue two of my books with beautiful covers by Fairfield. We will see. All I know is that when Fairfield picked me up at the hospital in New Haven on the first day of summer in 1961 he said, "I'll never let you down, Jimmy." He never did and I am not about to let him down, no, it matters not that my dearest friend has been dead for ten years: a debt is a debt and must be paid.

54

Across the street a window goes rather blue: earliest glimmer of dawn, at seven in the morning, so much later, it seems, than it recently was. I can't wait for daylight savings to end.

JAMES SCHUYLER was born in 1923. He wrote five collections of poetry, in addition to *May 24th or So,* an early book of his poems published in 1966 by Tibor de Nagy Editions. He was also the author of three novels, one of them, *Nest of Ninnies,* written in collaboration with John Ashbery. In 1983 Mr. Schuyler was elected a Fellow of the Academy of American Poets. His many honors include a Guggenheim Fellowship, grants from the Ingram Merrill Foundation, and the Pulitzer Prize for Poetry for *The Morning of the Poem* in 1981. He died in 1991.

DARRAGH PARK received degrees from Yale and Columbia Universities. He has had eleven solo exhibitions in New York since 1980. His paintings have been included in numerous group exhibitions and museum shows throughout the United States, including the Heckscher Museum, the Butler Institute of American Art and the Polk Museum of Art. He has had long associations with poets and has illustrated many poetry book covers including Schuyler's last four. Mr Park's fifth solo exhibition at the Tibor de Nagy Gallery was held in November 1995.

The text of this book is set in Goudy typeface.
One thousand copies were printed by McNaughton & Gunn, Inc.
in Saline, Michigan. *Two Journals* was edited by Eric Brown and
designed by Paul Lafortezza.